Study Guide: A Separate Peace

A Tolman Hall Literature Unit Study

RACHEL TOLMAN TERRY

TOLMAN HALL
LITERATURE UNIT STUDIES

Tolman Hall Literature Unit Studies allow you to customize your student's learning without having to do all the background work yourself. When you use Tolman Hall, you get all the resources you need to teach an in-depth literature unit, but you still have flexibility. If you want, you can focus your unit study on geography, or you can center your unit around a field trip. Even as you focus on one aspect of the literary work, your students will still learn about literary devices, vocabulary, and writing.

These unit studies are also ideal to use if you're teaching students of differing abilities. Since each unit study offers a variety of essay questions, projects, and vocabulary words, you can assign more difficult assignments to your advanced students, but everyone can still read and discuss the same literary work at the same time. This method of teaching the same literary enriches everyone's understanding of the story. Such discussions create common ground and cohesiveness and reduce the feelings of isolation students feel when they don't have anyone to talk to about what they're learning.

Enjoy learning with your students as you teach them with Tolman Hall Homeschool Literature Unit Studies. You'll prepare them for their future academic studies and get a chance to talk about ideas that add meaning to life.

CONTENTS

HOW TO USE THIS BOOK

If you don't wish to write in this book, photocopy the pages designated for vocabulary/spelling, reading quizzes, and short essay questions. This method works especially well if you're teaching the unit to more than one student at a time. Alternatively, you can dictate the questions to your students, which gives them additional handwriting and spelling practice. The answers to the reading quizzes are found at the back of the book.

INTRODUCTION

Tolman Hall Literature Unit Studies are designed to give you the flexibility to customize your own curriculum based on your students' interests while still providing a solid foundation in literature. If used as designed, students will learn and understand the literary concepts essential for doing well on standardized tests such as the SAT Literature Subject Test and the ACT Reading Test. Even more important, Tolman Hall Literature Studies will open their eyes to ideas, concepts, and deeper meanings that they may previously have skimmed over in cursory literature studies and in their reading for pleasure.

Each unit study provides background information about the author, several possible unit study schedules, a plot overview, and individual lessons. The lessons each contain a reading assignment, a summary and analysis of the assignment, a vocabulary lesson, a reading quiz, and short essay questions. Depending on your needs and schedule, you can customize the lessons to fit your students' needs. As the teacher, you can read along with your students, or if you're short on time, you can keep up by simply reading the summaries and analyses of each lesson, which give enough information for you to discuss the assignment with your student.

Many homeschooling parents teach more than one student at a time, and with Tolman Hall Unit Studies, you can teach the same work of literature at several grade levels. For instance, you could assign the same reading to students in grades 7 and 9 but assign the 9th grader more difficult writing assignments and more mature end-of-unit projects. In this way, your whole family can discuss the same books and authors while still meeting grade-appropriate requirements.

To help you use this unit study to the fullest, let's look at how to use each part of the curriculum.

Introduction to the Literary Work

Although it's sometimes fun to pick up a random library book and just begin reading, your student will gain a deeper understanding of the material with a formal introduction. The introduction generally includes information about the text: when it was written, how it came to be, and whether or not the literary work has been influential since it was published. You can read this introduction to your students, or give the information to your students and have them do further research on the Internet before presenting an introduction to *you*.

Schedule

Even though you can be more flexible in your scheduling, it's wise to set up a schedule for your literature unit study so your students get into a rhythm and know what's expected of them.

Each Tolman Hall Literature Unit Study suggests at least two different schedules for the unit study in an effort to meet different needs. Some unit studies will be shorter, and some will be longer, depending on the difficulty and length of the book. Feel free to adapt these schedules or compose your own using the different components in the unit study.

The Author

Learning about a work's author lends additional insight into the work itself, so each unit study includes biographical information about the author. If the author is still alive, you may also be able to find additional information (or even social media feeds!) that give you more personal, updated information. Discuss the author's biographical information with your students before you assign any reading. Your students may take a liking to particular authors; encourage this "relationship" by planning future literature unit studies with other books by the same author.

Plot Overview

Use your discretion with the plot overview included in each unit study guide. In most cases, it's not necessary to share this information with your students before beginning the unit, but it's very helpful for the teacher to have a larger picture, especially if you won't be reading along with your students.

Characters

The Characters section of the unit study will be most helpful to you, the teacher. As you discuss the book with your students, you may need to refer to the list of characters from time to time. Your students may find it helpful, too, however, especially if they create projects around the story's characters.

Lessons

Each lesson contains a reading assignment, a summary and analysis of the assignment, vocabulary words, a reading comprehension quiz, and short essay questions.

Reading assignments for shorter books may be combined, but if you combine reading assignments, reduce the amount of vocabulary and short essay work expected in one day. When you assign vocabulary words, read them aloud to your students, and have them write the words down as they think they are spelled. If they spell the words incorrectly, your vocabulary lesson has just become a spelling lesson as well. Dictation is a very effective way of discovering words your students don't know how to spell. Once the words are correctly written down, have your students look up the words and write definitions. If you want to further reinforce your vocabulary portion of the lesson, ask your students to write sentences containing the new vocabulary words.

The reading quizzes at the end of the lesson accomplish several objectives. First, they help your students to read more carefully, knowing they will be quizzed on their reading. Second, your students' answers help you to identify misunderstandings that need to be cleared up. Third, your students will get more writing practice, especially if you instruct them to write their answers in complete sentences. The answers to the reading quizzes are found at the end of the book.

Each lesson ends with three short essay questions. Short essay questions are excellent practice for helping your students to write critically and effectively. Your students' first question will probably be, "How long does my answer have to be?" That's up to you, but as a general rule, tell your students that it needs to be long enough to make a clear, opinionated statement that is backed up by recognized facts and evidence from the text. Instruct your students to get right to the point without rewriting the question and then to answer the question in specific terms. Your student should avoid using generalizations (look for words like "all," "every," and "no one" to track down generalizations), and they should be prepared to defend every statement they make. Assigning all three short essay questions for each lesson may be too much for your students. At least at the beginning, choose the short essay question that is most applicable to your students (if you're teaching more than one student, consider assigning different questions to each student and then discussing their answers as a group), and demand excellent work.

Use of Literary Devices and Terms

After the Lessons portion of the unit study, you'll find a list of literary devices and terms, which are essential for middle school and high school students to know. These terms are used on the SAT Literature Subject Test and the ACT Reading Test.

Each literary device is explained in general and then specifically identified in the text your students just read. It may be overwhelming to discuss all of the literary devices and terms for a particular work, especially if your students are unfamiliar with most of them. If this is the case, focus on two or three literary devices until your students have a solid understanding of what they are and how they're used. For example, if you want your students to learn about similes and metaphors, review these two sections together and then assign your students a simple project to reinforce that learning. They could make posters showing the similes and metaphors included in the text or a clay sculpture representing an important symbol from the book.

End-of-unit Project Options

A successful literature unit will leave an impression on your students, especially if it ends with a memorable project. Each unit study gives you several end-of-unit project options to choose from; many of these projects will cross over into other academic subjects such as art, history, or geography. Choose the project that best meets your teaching objectives, and plan your schedule accordingly.

Best Wishes

Enjoy the time you and your students spend together reading and discussing great works of literature. Through your teaching and learning, you will broaden your horizons, meet interesting characters and people, and introduce your students to cultures and ideas with much to offer. Best wishes to you!

Introduction to *A Separate Peace*

A Separate Peace follows two friends, Gene and Phineas, through their last year at an all-boys New England prep school. Set during World War II, the boys vacillate between childhood and adulthood and between peace and war. During summer term, Phineas falls out of a tree, and his leg sustains a terrible injury. They grapple with the ramifications of a life changed by circumstance as they drift toward the war and all that lies ahead.

Published in 1960, *A Separate Peace* won the William Faulkner Foundation Award and Rosenthal Award of the National Institute of Arts and Letters, both in 1961.

Schedules

When planning your schedule for *A Separate Peace,* consider your students' ages and abilities. Use one of the following schedules or create your own to suit your needs.

Three-week General Schedule

Monday 1: Introduce book and author and read Lesson 1

Tuesday 1: Lesson 1 Reading Quiz, Vocabulary, one short essay question; Read Lesson 2

Wednesday 1: Lesson 2 Reading Quiz, Vocabulary, one short essay question; Read Lesson 3

Thursday 1: Lesson 3 Reading Quiz, Vocabulary, one short essay question; Read Lesson 4

Friday 1: Lesson 4 Reading Quiz, Vocabulary, one short essay question; Read Lesson 5

Monday 2: Lesson 5 Reading Quiz, Vocabulary, one short essay question; Read Lesson 6

Tuesday 2: Lesson 6 Reading Quiz, Vocabulary, one short essay question; Read Lesson 7

Wednesday 2: Lesson 7 Reading Quiz, Vocabulary, one short essay question; Read Lesson 8

Thursday 2: Lesson 8 Reading Quiz, Vocabulary, one short essay question; Read Lesson 9

Friday 2: Lesson 9 Reading Quiz, Vocabulary, one short essay question; Read Lesson 10

Monday 3: Lesson 10 Reading Quiz, Vocabulary, one short essay question; Read Lesson 11

Tuesday 3: Lesson 11 Reading Quiz, Vocabulary, one short essay question; Read Lesson 12

Wednesday 3: Lesson 12 Reading Quiz, Vocabulary, one short essay question; Read Lesson 13

Thursday 3: Lesson 13 Reading Quiz, Vocabulary, one short essay question

Friday 3: End-of-unit Projects

Four-week Writing Focus Schedule

Monday 1: Introduce book and author; Read Lesson 1

Tuesday 1: Lesson 1 Reading Quiz; 2 short essay questions; Read Lesson 2

Wednesday 1: Lesson 2 Reading Quiz; 2 short essay questions; Read Lesson 3

Thursday 1: Lesson 3 Reading Quiz; 2 short essay questions; Read Lesson 4

Friday 1: Lesson 4 Reading Quiz; 2 short essay questions; Read Lesson 5

Monday 2: Lesson 5 Reading Quiz; 2 short essay questions; Read Lesson 6

Tuesday 2: Lesson 6 Reading Quiz; 2 short essay questions; Read Lesson 7

Wednesday 2: Lesson 7 Reading Quiz; 2 short essay questions; Read Lesson 8

Thursday 2: Lesson 8 Reading Quiz; 2 short essay questions; Read Lesson 9

Friday 2: Lesson 9 Reading Quiz; 2 short essay questions; Read Lesson 10

Monday 3: Lesson 10 Reading Quiz; 2 short essay questions; Read Lesson 11

Tuesday 3: Lesson 11 Reading Quiz; 2 short essay questions; Read Lesson 12

Wednesday 3: Lesson 12 Reading Quiz; 2 short essay questions; Read Lesson 13

Thursday 3: Lesson 13 Reading Quiz; 2 short essay questions

Friday 3: Write rough draft of Unit Project Essay

Monday 4: Conference on rough drafts; revise; make final version of Unit Project Essay

Tuesday 4: Athletic Brochure Unit Project

Wednesday 4: Athletic Brochure Unit Project

Thursday 4: History Unit Project

Friday 4: History Unit Project

Four-week Cultural Study Schedule

Monday 1: Introduce book and author; Read Lesson 1

Tuesday 1: Discuss Lesson 1; Vocabulary for Lesson 1; Read Lesson 2

Wednesday 1: Discuss Lesson 2; Vocabulary for Lesson 2; Read Lesson 3

Thursday 1: Discuss Lesson 3; Vocabulary for Lesson 3; Read Lesson 4

Friday 1: Research summer in New England. What kinds of daytime and nighttime temperatures would the students at Devon experience? How much precipitation? Create a weather newscast for the day and night Finny and Gene spend at the ocean.

Monday 2: Discuss Lesson 4; Vocabulary for Lesson 4; Read Lesson 5;

Tuesday 2: Discuss Lesson 5; Vocabulary for Lesson 5; Read Lesson 6

Wednesday 2: Discuss Lesson 6; Vocabulary for Lesson 6; Read Lesson 7

Thursday 2: Discuss Lesson 7; Vocabulary for Lesson 7; Read Lesson 8

Friday 2: Research the Olympics. What sports were included in the 1936-1948 Olympic Games? Were any of them canceled because of World War II? Did the war change the Olympics in any way? How did U.S. Olympic athletes do? Who were the standouts?

Monday 3: Discuss Lesson 8 and the Olympic research from Friday; Vocabulary for Lesson 8; Read Lesson 9

Tuesday 3: Discuss Lesson 9; Vocabulary for Lesson 9; Read Lesson 10

Wednesday 3: Discuss Lesson 10; Vocabulary for Lesson 10; Read Lesson 11

Thursday 3: Discuss Lesson 11; Vocabulary for Lesson 11; Read Lesson 12

Friday 3: Watch World War II recruiting films (you can find many of these on YouTube) and talk about the extraordinary pressures, opportunities, and dangers faced by young men who were coming of age in the early 1940s.

Monday 3: Discuss Lesson 12; Vocabulary for Lesson 12; Read Lesson 13

Tuesday 3: Discuss Lesson 13; Vocabulary for Lesson 13

Wednesday 3: History or Mapmaking Unit Project

Thursday 3: History or Mapmaking Unit Project

Friday 3: Watch the 1972 feature film *A Separate Peace*. It was filmed at John Knowles' school, Phillips Exeter Academy.

The Author

Author John Knowles wrote many books, but *A Separate Peace* is by far his most beloved. He also worked as a reporter and drama critic for *The Hartford Courant* and served as associate editor for *Holiday*, a travel magazine.

Born in West Virginia in 1926, John Knowles entered an all-boys New England boarding school, Exeter, at age 15. He graduated in 1945 and earned a bachelor's degree from Yale in 1949.

A Separate Peace was a huge commercial success, allowing Knowles to focus exclusively on his writing. In 1972, Paramount Pictures adapted the novel for film.

John Knowles died in 2001 at the age of 75.

Plot Overview

During the summer of 1942, the all-boys Devon School holds its first-ever summer session. Gene Forrester, a quiet, intelligent boy, becomes close friends with Finny, the school's best athlete. That summer, the boys start a secret society based on the ritual of jumping from a tree branch into the Devon River.

Gene is jealous of Finny's impressive athletic abilities, and he thinks Finny must be jealous of his own academic record. He even starts to hate Finny, but he keeps up the appearance of friendship.

One day, Finny and Gene decide to jump off the tree branch together, but as they inch their way out on the limb, Gene bends his knees, shaking the branch, and Finny falls to the bank, shattering his leg. No one blames Gene for the accident, but when Finny's doctor tells Gene that Finny's athletic career is over, Gene feels intensely guilty.

Finny goes home to recover, and Gene starts the fall session alone. He struggles to find his place without Finny. World War II is heating up and feeling closer to home, especially when military recruiters begin visiting Devon School. One of their classmates, Leper Lepellier, enlists, but he suffers a breakdown and returns home. Leper's failure makes everyone else dread the inevitable war.

Brinker Hadley, the class politician, wants to prove or disprove suspicions that Gene may have been responsible for Finny's fall. He organizes a late-night tribunal and summons Gene and Finny without warning. Leper implicates Gene, and Finny rushes out of the room. In his hurry, he falls down a marble staircase, re-breaking his leg.

Gene sneaks to the infirmary to see Finny, but Finny sends him away. The next morning, the two friends talk. Gene apologizes, and Finny forgives him. In the afternoon, Finny dies in surgery when some bone marrow detaches from the bone and travels to his heart. Gene feels that Finny will always be a part of him. The rest of the boys graduate and enlist in the military. Gene reflects on the hostility that plagues human relationships; he believes Finny was the only person immune from the curse.

Characters

Phineas

Phineas is the best athlete at Devon School. He's handsome, honest, confident, and extremely likable. He loves life and never perceives anyone to be an enemy. He has a rare gift for engaging others and helping people to enjoy the sheer joy of living.

Gene Forrester

Gene is Finny's best friend. He's also the narrator and protagonist of *A Separate Peace*. Thoughtful and intelligent, Gene excels in academics but feels jealous of Finny's athletic abilities and winning nature. He proves to be an unreliable narrator when it comes to his own emotions.

Leper Lepellier

Leper is a mild, gentle young man from Vermont, a classmate of Gene and Finny's. Despite his quiet, peaceful nature, he's the first member of his class to enlist in the war. Military life pushes Leper past his limits, and he suffers a breakdown.

Brinker Hadley

The charismatic political leader of the senior class at Devon, Brinker prizes orderliness and organization. He cares a great deal about truth and justice. He also lets the war affect his attitude and involvement in activities. Brinker seems to develop a resentful attitude over the course of the book, especially toward the older generation.

Cliff Quackenbush

Cliff is the manager of the crew team, and he's generally unpopular at Devon due to his Germanic heritage and his tendency to act aggressively toward anyone he deems to be inferior.

Mr. Ludsbury

Mr. Ludsbury is the master responsible for Gene's dormitory. He wants to restore order and discipline after the chaotic summer session.

Dr. Stanpole

Devon's resident doctor, Dr. Stanpole is a caring man who wishes the younger generation didn't have to deal with the harsh realities of war. He operates on Finny after both accidents.

Mr. Patch-Withers

Mr. Patch-Withers is the substitute headmaster of Devon during the summer session. Under his influence, the students enjoy much more freedom.

LESSON 1

Reading Assignment

Read Chapter 1 . We're going to go with a character back to a place he hasn't seen for a long time. Have you ever visited a place that you haven't seen for a long time? Did you remember the smells and the sights and sounds of the place? What kinds of memories came back to you? Did the place look smaller than you remember it?

Chapter 1 Summary

The narrator of the story goes back to the private, New England all-boys' school he attended fifteen years previously. He describes the school in detail as he explores the buildings and surrounding fields, comparing the way it looks now to the way it looked when he was a student, during World War II.

The narrator speaks of the fear he felt when he attended the Devon School as a student, and he's searching for something. He eats lunch at the Devon Inn and then goes back to the school.

It's a cold, gray, November day, and the narrator seems apprehensive as he searches for the fearful sites. He explores several buildings and then walks out to the fields surrounding the school. Walking toward the river, the narrator notices fog and begins to feel cold. Finally, he finds what he's looking for: an old tree, seemingly feeble in its old age.

The action now switches to the past, when the narrator is a 16-year-old student at the Devon School. He's enjoying a long summer afternoon with his best friend Phineas, who has decided that this particular tree is perfect for climbing and then using as a platform for jumping into the river.

Phineas and the narrator jump into the river while the other boys watch. They play in the water and then wrestle in the field; they're having too much fun to make it to dinner on time. In the evening, they do their reading in their dorm room and enjoy the peaceful, relaxing atmosphere of their very comfortable lives.

Chapter 1 Analysis

This first chapter includes an important literary device, the flashback. At the beginning of the chapter, the narrator, whose name is not known to us at this time, nervously explores his old school. The weather is bleak, and the tone is fearful. Halfway through the chapter, the flashback takes us back to the narrator's youth, fifteen years earlier. The tone shifts dramatically. Instead of a bleak winter day, the flashback is set in a golden summertime. The characters seem happy, carefree, and utterly content with their lives. This flashback, with its contrasting tones, sets up a conflict. We know something dramatic happens, but we don't yet know what. The author has piqued our curiosity.

It's also important to note that the author doesn't name the narrator at this time. Although the action is written in the first person ("I"), the focus seems to be centered on a different character, Phineas.

By the end of the chapter, we know a great deal about Phineas—how he talks, what he says, how he behaves, and how others feel about him—but we don't know much about the first-person narrator. This clues us in to the importance of Phineas's character to the arc of the story.

Lesson 1 Vocabulary/Spelling

Look the following words up in a dictionary or online and learn their meanings and spellings:

varnish

capacious

irate

prodigious

droll

seigneur

matriarchal

salient

Challenge: Use the words "droll" and "irate" in a single sentence.

Use the words "varnish" and "seigneur" to ask an interesting question.

Lesson 1 Reading Quiz

1. How long has it been since the narrator was a student at the Devon School?

2. In what part of the United States is Devon located?

3. What object is the narrator looking for in the fields around the school?

4. Whose idea is it to jump from the tree into the water?

5. What meal do Phineas and the narrator miss?

Lesson 1 Short Essay Questions

1. The narrator visits his old school and observes that some things look the same and other things look different. Write about a time you visited a place you hadn't been to for a long time. What was the same? What was different? How had you changed since you'd last been there? What are some of your memories of that place?

2. The tone of the flashback is serious and intense. Write a short essay about the components that contribute to the intense tone. Be specific, and include items like allusions, imagery, and certain words and phrases.

3. How do you know that Phineas and the narrator are "the best of friends"? Give three specific examples that illustrate their friendship.

LESSON 2

Reading Assignment

Have you ever had a friend like Phineas? Have you known anyone who pushed you out of your comfort zone and didn't seem worried about what other people thought? If not, would you like a friend like Finny? Read Chapter 2 to learn more about this charismatic character.

Chapter 2 Summary

Mr. Prud'Homme, a temporary teacher for the summer, has noticed that the narrator and Finny missed dinner. Finny explains that they'd been swimming in the river and then wrestling, and then the sunset was so beautiful, and they had to see several friends on business. Even though it's a rule to go to dinner, Mr. Prud'Homme is so amused by Finny's explanation that he lets the infraction slide.

The narrator thinks the teachers are going easier on them than usual because they're thinking about the war and the draft and how these students have so little time left to be boys: "We reminded them of what peace was like, of lives which were not bound up with destruction."

Phineas receives a pink pullover shirt in the mail from his mother, and he wears it around school. No one else could get away with wearing such a thing, but Finny can get away with anything, and he tells everyone he's wearing it as an emblem to celebrate the fact that America has bombed Central Europe, which he heard on the radio.

In the afternoon, Mr. Patch-Withers and his wife host a tea at the Headmaster's house. Everyone is slightly stiff and uncomfortable during the event—everyone, that is, except for Phineas. As Phineas casually and confidently talks to the adults, Mrs.

Patch-Withers notices that Phineas has used his school tie as a belt. She and her husband are appalled, but Phineas explains how wearing his tie as a belt is really a tribute to the school, and before long he has them both laughing.

After the tea, Finny and the narrator swim in the river and decide to form a club called the "Super Suicide Society of the Summer Session." Finny suggests jumping into the river together to cement their partnership. As they walk out on the tree limb, the narrator temporarily loses his balance, but Finny steadies him, and then they both jump into the river. The narrator later realizes that Finny saved his life when he steadied him.

Chapter 2 Analysis

Chapter 2 further develops the characters of Phineas and the narrator, although we still don't know the narrator's name. Phineas seems to be able to talk himself out of any trouble. In fact, Mr. Prud'Homme and Mr. and Mrs. Patch-Withers seem absolutely charmed by Phineas. It seems he can do no wrong, even when he's breaking the rules.

Alliteration is a literary device often used in poetry to add interest to the sounds of the words. By using words that have the same beginning sounds, authors create auditory interest. The name "Super Suicide Society of the Summer Session" is a great example of alliteration. There are seven "s" sounds within seven words. It's fun to say. It sounds light-hearted, even though "suicide" is a heavy and ominous word. The juxtaposition of the alliteration with the meaning of "suicide" is reminiscent of the juxtaposition of the narrator's trip back to Devon as an adult.

Lesson 2 Vocabulary

Look the following words up in a dictionary or online and learn their meanings and spellings:

eloquence

commendable

truant

hernia

broadcloth

emblem

temperamental

guillotine

indignant

Lesson 2 Reading Quiz

1. How is Mr. Prud'Homme dressed? How is this different from the way Devon Masters usually dress?

2. What color is the shirt Phineas receives from his mother?

3. Phineas is excited that America has bombed which part of the world?

4. In what year does this story take place?

5. How do Phineas and the narrator cement their partnership as leaders of the Super Suicide Society of the Summer Session?

Lesson 2 Short Essay Questions

1. Write about Mr. Prud'Homme's and Phineas's conversation from Mr. Prud'Homme's point of view. What is he really thinking about when he asks the boys about having missed dinner? How does he feel about Phineas and his explanations?

2. Why do Mr. and Mrs. Patch-Withers respond the way they do to seeing how Phineas uses his school tie as a belt? Do you have any articles of clothing that your parents or teachers would be shocked to see you wear in a casual way? Do you think clothing expectations were different in 1942 than they are now? Why or why not?

3. The narrator says, "He got away with everything because of the extraordinary kind of person he was. It was quite a compliment to me, as a matter of fact, to have such a person choose me for his best friend." Have you ever felt proud of having a certain person as a friend? Why did you feel proud? Do you think your friend felt the same way?

LESSON 3

Reading Assignment

Read Chapter 3. How would you describe the mood of Devon's summer session?

Chapter 3 Summary

The Super Suicide Society of the Summer Session quickly gains followers. They meet every single night, and the meetings open with Gene and Finny jumping into the river from the tree limb. Gene gets tired of their nightly meetings, and he doesn't enjoy jumping from the tree branch into the river, but he goes along with it to please Finny.

One day, Finny creates a brand new sport with a heavy medicine ball. He calls it "blitzball," and he is very good at it. There are no teams in blitzball; it's every man for himself. Finny is better at blitzball than everyone else. "Blitzball" quickly becomes the hit of the summer. Gene believes that it's still played in some form at Devon School fifteen years later.

Gene reminisces about how the years of World War II become the reality of his life. Trains are always full of servicemen, money is easy to earn but hard to spend because of the rationing, and newspapers are always crowded with maps of foreign places with hard-to-pronounce names.

One day, Finny and Gene are alone at the school swimming pool, and Finny decides he wants to try to beat the 100-yard freestyle school swimming record. It's currently held by someone named A. Hopkins Parker. They find a stopwatch in the office, and Gene times Finny. He beats the record by .7 second. Finny asks Gene not to tell anyone about his breaking the record, and Gene is very impressed by this: "There was something inebriating in the suppleness of this feat. When I thought about it my head felt a little dizzy and my stomach began to tingle. It had, in one word, glamour, absolute schoolboy glamour." Then Finny says that swimming in pools is "screwy" and suggests they go to the beach.

The beach is hours away via bicycle, but they head out anyway, even though they risk expulsion. They get to the beach late in the afternoon and jump into the ocean. They eat hot dogs for dinner and then sleep on a sand dune. Finny tells Gene that he's his best pal.

Chapter 3 Analysis

Finny seems more and more invincible. He makes up a popular sport on the spot, he breaks the school swimming record on his first try and doesn't want to tell anybody about it, and he fragrantly breaks the rule about leaving campus. At the beach, people turn and stare at him because he's so good looking.

This is all intoxicating to Gene. At each step, he feels discomfort about Finny's behavior. He doesn't want to jump off the tree bough every night, but he does it so he doesn't disappoint Finny. He doesn't want to go to the beach because he needs to study for his test, but he goes anyway because he can't resist Finny's persuasiveness. This inner conflict is growing with each new situation.

The author takes a step back from the action in the middle of Chapter 3 to reflect on his life in high school. Clearly, Gene is back to his adult persona during his reflections. Although it doesn't say so, perhaps he's still walking the grounds of Devon during his visit that began at the start of Chapter 1. Regardless, the voice we hear in the middle of Chapter 3 is the voice of grown-up Gene, an older and wiser Gene thinking back to his youth. In addition to reminding us about the older Gene, this section gives us an acute sense of the setting. It reminds us who is president, what life looks like during the war, and what sights, sounds, and colors are present in the story. It helps us to understand the time and place of the story.

Lesson 3 Vocabulary

Look up the following words and phrases in a dictionary or online and learn their meanings and spellings:

catacomb

haphazard

cordial

calisthenics

blitzkrieg

shuttlecock

honky-tonk

monologue

Use the following two vocabulary words in a single sentence: "calisthenics" and "shuttlecock."

Lesson 3 Reading Quiz

1. How often does the Super Suicide Society of the Summer Session meet?

2. How often does Gene miss meetings of the Super Suicide Society?

3. How many teams are there in a game of blitzball?

4. Who is A. Hopkins Parker?

5. Name two reasons Gene doesn't want to ride bikes to the beach.

Lesson 3 Short Essay Questions

1. As the boys are discussing their new sport, Bobby Zane says, "Let's make it have something to do with the war." Why do you think they get excited about playing a new game that has something to do with the war?

2. In the middle of Chapter 3, the narrator gives us a vivid description of life in America during the war. Write a similar vivid description about a particular time and place in your life. Use concrete examples of sights, sounds, and smells.

3. Would you enjoy being friends with a person like Finny? Why or why not? Have you ever had a friend like Finny?

LESSON 4

Reading Assignment

Have you ever seen the sun rise? Gene sees it for the first time in Chapter 4, and he's surprised that it starts out as "a strange gray thing." Read Chapter 4.

Chapter 4 Summary

Gene wakes up on the sand dune before Finny does. He worries that he won't make it back to Devon in time for his test, especially when Finny wakes up and immediately goes swimming in the ocean. They don't have any more money, so they ride the three hours back on their bicycles with empty stomachs. Gene makes it back just in time for his test, but he flunks it.

They have a full day of blitzball and a meeting of the Super Suicide Society of the Summer Session, and as Gene works on his trigonometry that night, he has a realization: he believes that Finny is trying to prevent him from a successful student. Gene figures that they're equals because he's the best student in the school and Finny is the best athlete. If Finny can get him to compromise on his academic standards, then they won't be equals anymore. Finny will win. He starts to wonder if Finny planned the beach excursion just so Gene wouldn't have time to study for his test. He thinks the nightly club meetings and the long games of blitzball are calculated to distract him from studying. Their summer continues on, and they get along well, but Gene is skeptical of Finny's intentions.

It's now August, and exams for the summer term are approaching. One night, Gene is trying to study for his French exam when Finny comes in to announce that Leper Leppelier is going to jump from the tree to the river during the nightly meeting of the Super Suicide Society, and it's time to go watch him. Gene loses his patience and snaps that he's trying to study. Finny nonchalantly tells him it's no big deal—if Gene needs to stay home and study, he should study. Finny can supervise Leper. That's when Gene realizes that Finny hasn't been jealous. Gene is the one who has been jealous. And he'll never beat Finny because Finny is made of finer stuff.

Gene goes to the meeting, and Phineas suggests that the two of them do a double jump out of the tree. As they walk out on the limb, Gene's knees bend, jouncing the limb. Finny loses his balance, and he falls through the branches to the ground below.

Chapter 4 Analysis

The first paragraph of Chapter 4 contains an interesting simile. Similes are literary devices that help us to understand something by comparing it to something else. In this case, the author compares dawn to "sunshine seen through burlap." Perhaps we can't quite picture the dawn as the author sees it, but when it's described as "sunshine seen through burlap," we see what he's seeing.

The author's description of the dawn also contains an allusion, which is a reference to some other work of literature or art. "Phineas, still asleep on his dune, made me think of Lazarus, brought back to life by the touch of God." Lazarus is a character in the Bible. He is the brother of Mary and Martha, and all three of these siblings are friends of Jesus. Lazarus dies while Jesus is away for a few days, and as he comes back, Martha finds him on the road and tells him that Lazarus has died and if he had been there, he could have saved him. Jesus ends up raising Lazarus from the dead. Not only is this an allusion, but the image of Phineas as Lazarus is foreshadowing, a hint of something to come.

At this point in the novel, we've seen enough of Phineas to make our own assessments of him. We know that he's talented and likable, that he seems to enjoy Gene's friendship, and that he gets away with breaking rules on a regular basis. Now Gene is showing skepticism of Finny's motives. He thinks Finny is using the Super Suicide Society to distract Gene from his studying so he won't get good grades. He continues to go along with Finny's antics so Finny won't know that he knows.

On the evening that Leper Lepellier says he'll jump out of the tree, Gene is particularly irritated with being interrupted while he's trying to study. The author writes about Finny's fall in a way that leaves us wondering if Gene's wobble was an accident.

Lesson 4 Vocabulary

Look the following words up in a dictionary or online and learn their meanings and spellings:

fanfare

mordant

detonation

solace

enmity

effulgence

curt

menace

jounce

Lesson 4 Reading Quiz

1. Why don't Phineas and Gene eat breakfast when they wake up at the beach?

2. How does Gene do on his test when he gets back from the beach?

3. How does Mr. Prud'Homme react when Gene tells him about their excursion to the beach?

4. Why does Gene become angry when Phineas tells him they're going to go watch Leper Lepellier jump out of the tree?

5. What does Gene do immediately after Phineas falls?

Lesson 4 Short Essay Questions

1. Would you rather be roommates with Phineas or Gene? Explain your reasoning.

2. Explain why you think Gene believes this: "You and Phineas are even already. You are even in enmity. You are both coldly driving ahead for yourselves alone. You did hate him for breaking that school swimming record, but so what? He hated you for getting an A in every course but one last term. You would have had an A in that one except for him. Except for him." Do you think this statement is true? How has Gene come to believe this?

3. After Finny falls out of the tree, Gene says, "With unthinking sureness I moved out on the limb and jumped into the river, every trace of my fear of this forgotten." Why do you think Gene's fear is forgotten? Why does he feel so sure now?

LESSON 5

Reading Assignment

Read Chapter 5. Before you read, consider how Finny's accident might impact each of the characters.

Chapter 5 Summary

For several days, no one is allowed to see Phineas in the infirmary. Gene tries not to think too much about what happened. One night, he puts on Finny's clothes and looks in the mirror and is surprised to see how much he looks like his friend.

Then one morning Dr. Stanpole tells Gene that Phineas wants to see him. The doctor reports that Finny is doing much better and that he'll walk again but that sports are finished for him. Gene is shocked, but he tells the doctor he'll go visit Phineas in the infirmary. Dr. Stanpole tells him to be cheerful and hopeful for Finny's sake.

When Gene visits Phineas in the infirmary, he's surprised to see that Finny looks physically diminished. Finny is glad to see him and gracious. Gene feels compelled to tell Finny that he jostled the branch on purpose, but just before he gets a chance, a nurse comes in and sends him away. The next day the doctor decides Finny isn't well enough for visitors, and then the Summer Session ends and everyone goes home.

Finny is taken to his home outside of Boston in an ambulance, and Gene goes home to the South.

After a month of vacation, everyone returns to Devon. On his way back to school, Gene stops in Boston to see Finny. He has never seen Finny in his home before. All of his interactions with him had been in their impersonal dorm room or at school. He still feels he must tell Finny, and he does: "I was thinking about you and the accident because I caused it… I deliberately jounced the limb so you would fall off."

Finny responds by saying, "Of course you didn't do it," but Gene won't let it go. Finally, Gene notices that he's injuring Phineas again, and that this injury might be even deeper than the original injury. Now he wonders if he really did it on purpose or not.

Gene leaves to go back to school, and Phineas says he'll be there by Thanksgiving. As Gene leaves, Phineas says, "You aren't going to start living by the rules, are you?" And Gene responds, "Oh no, I wouldn't do that."

Chapter 5 Analysis

The bulk of Chapter 5 consists of two separate conversations between Gene and Finny. Both conversations are focused on the same topic: the accident. Gene wants to confess that he caused the accident. Finny seems to sense that this was the case, but he doesn't want to believe it.

While much of the character development at the beginning of the novel was focused on Phineas (remember, we didn't even know Gene's name in the first few chapters), now it seems that the author is focusing more on the development of Gene's character. Even in his tragedy, Phineas is trying to console his friend and help him to feel better. Gene, on the other hand, doesn't seem to have the capacity to look outside himself enough to be careful about Finny's feelings. He's more concerned with the relief he'll feel when he tells the truth than he is with how his suffering friend will respond to the truth.

The setting changes in this chapter as well. Until now, all of the action, including the episode in the first chapter when Gene visits his old school as an adult, has taken place in or near Devon. Now we see Phineas and Gene in a totally different environment, Finny's home outside of Boston. The family pictures and and comfortable furniture in Finny's home allows us to see him in a different light. He's a member of a family, somebody's son, not just a start athlete at a prestigious boys' school. A new setting can help us to understand a character or an event in a new way.

Chapter 5 ends with a bit of foreshadowing: "I grinned at him. 'Oh no, I wouldn't do that,' and that was the most false thing, the biggest lie of all." Gene is about to return to Devon School, and he'll be there for a couple of months before Phineas returns. We readers don't yet know why it's a big lie for Gene to say that he won't start living by the rules. We'll have to read on to find out why. This foreshadowing hints at big things to come.

Lesson 5 Vocabulary

Look the following words up in a dictionary or online and learn their meanings and spellings:

cordovan

aristocrat

grandee

recessional

infirmary

transfix

reverie

ell

Use the words "cordovan" and "transfix" in a single sentence.

Lesson 5 Reading Quiz

1. What does Gene wear that makes him feel like "some Spanish grandee"?

2. What advice does Dr. Stanpole give to Gene before he visits Finny in the infirmary?

3. What story does Gene tell Finny about what happened down South during his visit?

4. What does Gene tell Finny about the accident?

5. Will Gene make it back to Devon on time?

Lesson 5 Short Essay Questions

1. At first, Gene worries that people will be suspicious of him, and he tries to develop the strength to defend himself against accusations. But no accusations come. Why does he feel so guilty? Do you think he should feel guilty? Why or why not?

2. Gene tries on Finny's clothes, and when he looks at himself in the mirror he sees "Phineas, Phineas to the life." What is happening inside of Gene as he tries on Finny's clothes and sees himself as Finny? Have you ever dressed differently than you normally do and felt like a completely different person? Do clothes have the power to change the way we see ourselves or how other people see us?

3. In an instant, Finny's life has changed forever. Compare and contrast the way Phineas and Gene deal with Finny's injury. What do we learn about these two characters based on the way they cope with the accident?

LESSON 6

Reading Assignment

How does your life change when summer ends and fall begins? Read Chapter 6 and notice the many changes at Devon School.

Chapter 6 Summary

The first Summer Session in Devon's history is over, and the 163rd Winter Session begins. Along with the masters and students, tradition and order returns to the school. Everyone assembles in the chapel for the opening meeting, and Gene feels that everything has changed, even though "continuity" is the theme of all the sermons, hymns, and announcements.

As he sits through the meeting, Gene thinks about how the summer changed everything. Traditions were broken, and standards were let down and forgotten. Most of all, Phineas had been forever changed.

After the service, all 700 students rush out into the cool air, scurrying to get to appointments and classes on time. Leper no longer lives across the hall from Gene. He's been moved to a building somewhere over by the old gym. Brinker Hadley, one of the school's most powerful and persuasive students, has taken Leper's place.

After morning classes and lunch, Gene hurries down to the Crew House because he has signed up to be the assistant crew manager. On his way to the Crew House, Gene sees the Devon River and pictures Finny balancing on one foot on the prow of a canoe, one of his favorite tricks. Further down, Gene sees the Naguamsett, the ugly, saline lower river, which the boys never used during the summer.

At the Crew House, Gene meets Cliff Quackenbush, the crew manager. Although Cliff is a senior like Gene, he looks and seems older. He chastises Gene for being late and treats him scornfully. They start arguing, and when Cliff accuses Gene of being "maimed," Gene hits him hard across the face. They start wrestling and both end up in the Naguamsett.

On his way back to his dorm room to change, Gene runs into Mr. Ludsbury. The teacher has heard about the Summer Session, how the boys played poker in the dormitory and brought a leaky icebox into their room. Mr. Ludsbury tells him there's a phone call for him.

Gene goes to Mr. Ludsbury's study, expecting to hear that someone in his family is sick, and he's pleased to hear Finny's cheerful voice on the end of the line. Phineas called to make sure his spot has been saved in Gene's room and to hear how things are going. He tells Gene that if he can't play sports, then Gene will do it for him. He's shocked and disgusted to hear Gene planned on being the assistant crew manager. Gene realizes this is his opportunity to "become a part of Phineas."

Chapter 6 Analysis

The two rivers that straddle the Devon school are symbols. By learning about these symbols early on in the story, the entire plot will make more sense and take on more meaning.

The Devon is a narrow little river with a "thick fringe of pine and birch." It's a freshwater river, and its source lies just up the hill. When Gene sees the Devon, he thinks of "Phineas in exaltation, balancing on one foot on the prow of a canoe like a river god, his raised arms invoking the air to support him, face transfigured, body a complex set of balances and compensation…" The Devon is small, clean, and completely understood. It's predictable and safe. It's a symbol of youth and safety.

The Naguamsett, on the other hand, is "ugly, saline, fringed with marsh, mud and seaweed." It joins with the ocean, "so that its movements [are] governed by unimaginable factors like the Gulf Stream, the Polar Ice Cap, and the moon." It symbolizes adulthood and the unknown.

Youth is inevitably followed by adulthood, as the rivers suggest: "The Devon's course was determined by some familiar hills a little inland; it rose among highland farms and forests which we knew, passed at the end of its course through the school grounds, and then threw itself with little spectacle over a small waterfall beside the diving dam, and into the turbid Naguamsett."

It's the first day of Winter Session, and Phineas is far away. Gene's first conversation with another student is hostile, and when he gets into a fight with Cliff Quackenbush, they both end up in the dirty waters of the Naguamsett. Forces that Gene doesn't understand are throwing him into the adult world where he feels "unfriendly" and "shriveled."

Just in time, though, Gene receives a phone call from Finny. Optimism returns, and Gene feels a "soaring sense of freedom."

Lesson 6 Vocabulary

Look the following words up in a dictionary or online and learn their meanings and spellings:

stopgap

sultry

keynote

idiosyncratic

wit

infinitesimal

sinecure

squall

icebox

Lesson 6 Reading Quiz

1. Who had lived across the hall from Gene and Phineas during the Summer Session?

2. What is the difference between the two rivers on the Devon School property?

3. What is Gene's last name?

4. Who is Cliff Quackenbush?

5. Why does Phineas call Gene on the phone?

Lesson 6 Short Essay Questions

1. Describe at least three differences between the Summer Session and the Winter Session. What does Gene miss about the Summer Session?

2. The two rivers on the Devon School property are symbols. Describe what they could symbolize and how they fit into the story.

3. Just before they begin fighting, Gene says, "You, Quackenbush don't know anything about who I am." This is probably true, but do you think Gene knows himself at this point in the story? What does it mean to "find yourself"? Has Gene found himself? Or is he still searching? What do you think he needs to do in order to "know himself"?

LESSON 7

Reading Assignment

Read Chapter 7. Although Gene has attended the Devon School for years, everything feels different at the start of this Winter Session. Are there times when your familiar surroundings feel different?

Chapter 7 Summary

Gene changes out of his sticky, salty clothes and puts on a pair of pants Phineas had frequently worn. Brinker Hadley comes in and jovially teases Gene about knocking off his roommate so he can have a room all to himself. This makes Gene uncomfortable. To escape the discomfort, he suggests they head down to the Butt Room.

The Butt Room is a dungeon-like room in the basement where the students gather to smoke and chat. To discourage smoking, the administrators have made the room as depressing as possible, but the boys still like to hang out there.

Brinker continues his joke and acts like Gene is a criminal being prosecuted for killing his roommate. They all want to know what happened to Finny. Gene tries to play along casually, saying he started to slip arsenic into Finny's morning coffee. But that's not good enough for Brinker, who wants Gene to admit that he pushed Finny out of the tree.

After floundering, Gene finally starts to regain control of the conversation by making fun of a younger boy in the room. "He had a very weak foothold among the Butt Room crowd, and I had pretty well pushed him off it." He can tell that the younger boy hates him now, but he was willing to pay that price to escape the group's scrutiny.

The war seems far away and boring. The boys help to pick the local apple crop because the harvesters have all gone into the army or the war factories. Then winter comes early with a series of heavy snowfalls. The trains at the local depot become stuck on the tracks, and the Devon boys go to help dig them out.

On his way to the train station, Gene sees Leper in a meadow not far from the river. Gene hasn't talked with Leper since the Winter Session began, but Leper talks to him as if no time has passed. Leper is wearing cross-country skis, which he calls "touring skis," and he is looking for a beaver dam he wishes to photograph. Gene and Leper talk about skiing. Leper feels that downhill skiing is ruining skiing because people don't have time to slow down and look at things. Gene wishes him well and heads to the station.

The work at the train station is arduous, dirty, and loud. One of the trains is filled with young servicemen, not much older than the Devon students themselves. They're wearing fresh new uniforms, and they seem to be having a wonderful time. On the way back to the school, Quackenbush says he'll finish out the year at school and then sign up for the army. Someone accuses him of being a German spy.

They come across Leper. He is happy and satisfied; he found the beaver dam in one of the tributaries of the Devon. Brinker is exasperated that his classmates consist of "draft-dodging Kraut" and a "photographer of beaver dams." He announces that he's going to enlist the very next day.

Gene feels exhilarated by Brinker's announcement and starts to think that he'll do the same thing. He's ready for a change, and the army will be just the change he needs. He bounds up the stairs to his room and sees light emanating from under the door. Phineas is back.

Chapter 7 Analysis

A powerful force exerts itself in this chapter, and not one character can do anything to resist its influence. That powerful force is World War II, which makes demands on every character in the story. The Devon students interrupt their studies to harvest apples and dig trains out of the snow.

One character, however, is doing his very best to ignore the war. While his classmates volunteer their labor at the train station and become swept up in the excitement of the conflict, Leper puts on his old-fashioned skis and heads up to one of the Devon's tributaries to look for a beaver dam. Consider the symbolism of Leper's trek. If the Devon River symbolizes childhood and innocence, what do its tributaries symbolize? And what is the function of dams? Leper is trekking as far into innocence as possible to find out how beavers build dams. He doesn't want the water to flow down the river and dump into the Naguamsett because the Naguamsett is unpredictable, messy adulthood, and it's frightening.

When Brinker teases Gene about trying to kill off his roommate so he can have the entire dorm room to himself, Gene becomes defensive and uncomfortable. His discomfort is magnified down in the Butt Room when the others want to hear details of Finny's accident. In fact, Gene is so uncomfortable, that he makes fun of a younger student in order to deflect attention away from himself. We know from the way Gene treats Leper that he is ordinarily a very kind person. His treatment of the younger student is not characteristic of him.

Gene begins to think there's something wrong with himself: "there was always something deadly lurking in anything I wanted, anything I loved. And if it wasn't there, as for example with Phineas, then I put it there myself." He makes this comment as he contemplates joining the army right away, as Brinker proposes to do. Gene clearly blames himself for Finny's accident.

Before we even see that Phineas is back, the author provides some subtle foreshadowing: the light "poured in a thin yellow slab of brightness from under the door, illuminating the dust and splinters of the hall floor." Phineas brings light and life to everyone he touches.

Lesson 7 Vocabulary

Look the following words up in a dictionary or online and learn their meanings and spellings:

genial

insinuating

treachery

fratricide

galvanize

arsenic

funereal

contretemps

burlesque

Lesson 7 Reading Quiz

1. Describe Brinker Hadley's appearance and personality.

2. What is the Butt Room?

3. What agricultural chore do the Devon students perform because of the worker shortage?

4. What is Leper looking for when Gene runs into him on the ridge?

5. Why do the Devon students go to the train station?

Lesson 7 Short Essay Questions

1. Leper says, "They're ruining skiing in this country, rope tows and chair lifts and all that stuff. You get carted up, and then you whizz down. You never get to see the trees or anything. Oh you see a lot of trees shoot by, but you never get to really look at trees, at a tree. I just like to go along and see what I'm passing and enjoy myself." What other changes are happening in the United States during World War II that could be compared to the changes Leper notices in skiing?

2. After the Devon students finish digging out the railyard, Gene makes this observation: "Stranded in this mill town railroad yard while the whole world was converging elsewhere, we seemed to be nothing but children playing among heroic men." Have you ever felt that you were a child "playing among heroic men"? Describe that time and how you responded.

3. Leper has been looking for a beaver dam in one of the Devon River's tributaries. What could Leper, the beaver dam, and the tributaries symbolize? Leper says the beaver didn't reveal himself. What could the beaver symbolize?

LESSON 8

Reading Assignment

How do you think things will change now that Finny has returned to Devon? Will Gene and Brinker still enlist?

Chapter 8 Summary

With his crutches and cast, Phineas looks like an injured athlete, not an uncommon sight at Devon. He complains about the lack of maids, and Gene makes up the bed for him. With Finny back, Gene figures it's time to start saying his bedtime prayers again, and they wait for each other to finish before Finny starts talking in the dark.

The next morning, Brinker comes bounding in, talking about enlisting, but Finny can't believe they were even considering it, and soon, talk of enlistment becomes a joke. In fact, Brinker even earns a nickname, The Yellow Peril, in the joke about enlisting. It's the first time Brinker has had a nickname, and it sticks with him until graduation.

With Phineas back, peace has returned to Devon for Gene. That first morning of Finny's return, Finny convinces Gene to skip morning classes with him. It's an icy day, and the campus is dangerous for Finny on his crutches. Still, they trek the quarter mile to the gym where Finny confesses that he had been planning on trying out for the 1944 Olympics. Gene mentions that there won't be any Olympics because of the war, and Finny can't believe that Gene has bought in to the war conspiracy. The conspiracy is concocted, Finny explains, by a bunch of fat old men who want to keep all the steak and fuel for themselves. It's a way of keeping the young people of the 1940s in line, just as the Depression reined in the kids of the 1930s. Anyhow, Finny continues, since he can't compete in the 1944 Olympics, Gene will have to do it instead. He orders Gene to start doing chin-ups. Gene has ever only done twelve chin-ups in the past, but somehow, with Finny counting for him, he does thirty.

All through the semester, Finny helps Gene with his athletic training, and Gene helps Finny with his studies. One morning, as Gene runs around the icy walk during his morning training, he experiences something he's never felt before. He had been on the point of exhaustion when, suddenly, he feels magnificent and energetic. As they walk back to the dorm, they run into Mr. Ludsbury, who thinks they're training for the military. Finny is surprised that Mr. Ludsbury really thinks there's a war on. Then he realizes why: "Too thin. Of course."

Chapter 8 Analysis

With Phineas back at Devon, Gene gratefully falls back into his old ways: saying his prayers before falling asleep and following Finny's lead, wherever it takes him. The chapter is full of symbolism, as we see the conflicts between Finny's idealistic world and the war, which is encroaching on the boys' lives.

When Brinker explains that he was going to enlist, Finny doesn't respond. Instead, he grabs his soap dish and says, "I'm first in the shower." He hasn't been working at the train station like the other boys. He hasn't been covered in soot and sweat, and yet, he's the one who wants to wash himself clean. He needs something to wash the war-time world away.

Finny's cast symbolizes reality. It is heavy and cumbersome, and he can't shake it off. When Finny gets ready to go to the shower, Brinker asks, "You can't get that cast wet, can you?" Finny replies, "No, I'll keep it outside the curtain." Brinker: "I'll help." Finny can't completely get rid of reality, but he can "keep it outside the curtain," pretending that it doesn't exist. The other boys help Finny to ignore reality by playing along with his fantasies and games.

An extended metaphor helps readers to understand the impact of the war: "So the war swept over like a wave at the seashore, gathering power and size as it bore on us, overwhelming in its rush, seemingly inescapable, and then at the last moment eluded by a word from Phineas; I had simply ducked, that was all, and the wave's concentrated power had hurtled harmlessly overhead, no doubt throwing others roughly up on the beach, but leaving me peaceably treading water as before. I did not stop to think that one wave is inevitably followed by another even larger and more powerful, when the tide is coming in."

Several allusions add meaning to Chapter 8. These allusions would have been familiar to 1944's prep school students. As Gene recounts the hazards on campus for Phineas, he describes the school's architecture as "a peculiar style of Puritan grandeur, as though Versailles had been modified for the needs of a Sunday School." Versailles is the opulent palace of King Louis XXIV.

And Mr. Ludsbury alludes to Napoleon Bonaparte's historic battle loss when he says, "…all exercise today is aimed of course at the approaching Waterloo." Finny rejects Mr. Ludsbury's suggestion with a flat, "No," refusing to acknowledge the existence of the war.

Lesson 8 Vocabulary

Look the following words up in a dictionary or online and learn their meanings and spellings:

clodhopper

ambiguous

indignant

senatorial

appalled

inevitable

elude

reticent

bric-á-brac

Lesson 8 Reading Quiz

1. Who gives Brinker Hadley his new nickname of "Yellow Peril"?

2. Why is Devon dangerous for Finny in the winter?

3. What is Finny's opinion about the war?

4. Phineas has a goal for Gene. What is the goal?

5. What does Mr. Ludsbury look like?

Lesson 8 Short Essay Questions

1. Gene recollects, "Around Devon we had gaits of every description; gangling shuffles from boys who had suddenly grown a foot taller, swinging cowboy lopes from those thinking of how wide their shoulders had become, ambles, waddles, light trippings, gigantic Bunyan strides. But Phineas had moved in continuous flowing balance, so that he had seemed to drift along with no effort at all, relaxation on the move." Think of five people you know well and describe in detail how they walk. Use descriptive words and even similes, metaphors, and allusions ("Bunyan strides") to describe their gaits.

2. This chapter contains several allusions to important figures in the World War II era. Find information about Elliott Roosevelt, Madame Chiang Kai-shek, and General MacArthur. Then explain in a short essay who they are and why the boys say, "I wouldn't enlist with you if you were Elliott Roosevelt (or Madame Chiang Kai-sheck or General MacArthur's son).

3. Do you think Phineas really doesn't believe the war is real? How could he not believe it's real? Why does Gene play along with Finny's assertion?

LESSON 9

Reading Assignment

Read Chapter 9 and think about the differences between Leper's life in the military and his classmates' reveling back at the Devon School.

Chapter 9 Summary

Leper Lepellier decides to enlist after a recruiter from the United States ski troops shows a film to the whole senior class. He's the first member of the class to leave, and he becomes the boys' link to the war. When they hear news items about the war, they automatically link Leper to the event: "We talked about Leper's stand at Stalingrad, Leper on the Burma Road, Leper's convoy to Archangel…"

On a late winter Saturday afternoon, Phineas organizes a Winter Carnival to lift everyone's spirits. He makes assignments, and everyone goes along with his plans. They manage to procure some hard cider, prizes for the games, music, and a ski jump. They build snow sculptures and start the Carnival by burning a copy of the Iliad.

As the boys drink the hard cider, the carnival spins out of control with boys soaring through the air off the ski jump, knocking the heads off statues, and making music. In the midst of the ruckus, Phineas climbs up on the prize table and starts dancing. "It was his wildest demonstration of himself, of himself in the kind of world he loved; it was his choreography of peace."

Brownie Perkins arrives from the dormitory with a telegram for Gene. Finny shouts that it must be from the Olympic Committee, but it's really from Leper. It says, "I

HAVE ESCAPED AND NEED HELP. I AM AT CHRISTMAS LOCATION. YOU UNDERSTAND. NO NEED TO RISK ADDRESS HERE. MY SAFETY DEPENDS ON YOU COMING AT ONCE."

Chapter 9 Analysis

The theme of peace runs through Chapter 9. Gene begins by talking about his lapse into Finny's "vision of peace." He's able to ignore the confusion all around him because "peace is indivisible," and he doesn't have to try to make sense of the world around him.

Note the wonderful example of alliteration in the third paragraph of the chapter: "Nothing tainted these white warriors of winter…" The soothing sound of the w's matches the tone of the film shown to the boy by the ski troops recruiter.

The Winter Carnival is another of Finny's fantasies to help keep the war at bay. The many preparations keep the boys busy, and they all enjoy themselves immensely. The end of Chapter 9 highlights the irreconcilable differences between childhood and adulthood, between innocence and knowledge, between peace and war. Phineas has healed enough to get up on the table and dance. "Phineas recaptured that magic gift for existing primarily in space, one foot conceding briefly to gravity its rights before spinning him off again into the air." He is again at the height of his powers, but that level of innocence and peace cannot coexist with the stark reality of a world war. As soon as he finishes his "choreography of peace," Brownie Perkins arrives with a telegram. The first enlistee from Devon has failed. Something has gone terribly wrong.

Lesson 9 Vocabulary

Look the following words up in a dictionary or online and learn their meanings and spellings:

indivisible

vagary

liaison

incompetent

cinder

garrison

hard cider

encroachment

illusory

Lesson 9 Reading Quiz

1. Who is the first member of the class to enlist?

2. What are Saturday afternoons like in a boys' school in winter?

3. What event does Phineas create to enliven the atmosphere?

4. Which of the prizes does Phineas "sacrifice" in order to have a fire?

5. Gene receives a telegram during the carnival. Who is it from?

Lesson 9 Short Essay Questions

1. Leper says, "I'm almost glad this war came along. It's like a test, isn't it, and only the things and the people who've been evolving the right way survive. Based on what you've read so far, which characters are "evolving the right way" to survive?

2. If you were in charge of the Winter Carnival, what events, refreshments, and decorations would you plan for? Remember that you don't have any money to spend.

3. What is significant about the Winter Carnival taking place on the bank of the Naguamsett River? Mention at least two specifics.

LESSON 10

Reading Assignment

The setting changes dramatically in Chapter 10, and the narrator (older Gene) offers some interesting information about the future.

Chapter 10 Summary

Gene immediately embarks on a journey to Leper's home in northern Vermont. It's a bleak, drafty train ride, and when he finally reaches the depot at dawn, he has to walk to the Lepelliers' house outside of town.

As Gene approaches the house, he can see Leper watching him from one of the windows. As usual, Leper dispenses with formalities and small talk and dives right into the middle of a conversation about the usefulness of dining rooms. Gene tries to make a joke, but Leper doesn't appreciate it. He seems agitated and nearly cries over a simple comment about mealtime.

Gene asks how long Leper will be home, and Leper explains that he escaped the army because they were going to give him a Section Eight discharge. A Section Eight discharge means the person is mentally unfit, and Leper fears he will never be able to get a job because of the stigma.

He doesn't sound like himself ("None of this could have been said by the Leper of the beaver dam"). He becomes hostile and accusatory, and he repeatedly calls Gene a savage, reminding him of "that time you knocked Finny out of the tree." At this, Gene kicks the legs of the stool Leper sits in, and Leper's mother rushes in to see what's wrong.

Gene apologizes, and Leper invites him to stay for lunch. He does, but only because he's too ashamed to leave. Gene eats heartily, and this seems to win Mrs. Lepellier's approval. When they finish eating, Leper and Gene go for a walk.

Glistening, crusted snow covers the landscape, and the sun shines brightly. The snow cracks under their feet as they walk. Leper tells Gene about the army and how everything is inside out. While in the military, he couldn't sleep at night, and he couldn't eat at mealtime. Leper began to hallucinate during his classes and in the barracks. He describes his horrible hallucinations in grisly detail, and Gene can't stand it anymore. He tells Leper to shut up, and he runs down the road away from the house and goes back to Devon.

Chapter 10 Analysis

If Phineas represents childhood and innocence, Leper takes simplicity one step further. He is naive and wholly unacquainted with the realities of the adult world and the war. The author helps us to understand this with the scene about the beaver dam. Leper has missed the announcement about clearing snow from the train depot. So while the other boys get grimy and dirty, assisting the soldiers in getting to the war, Leper skis through the pristine snow up to one of the tributaries of the Devon River. He's looking for a beaver dam. He wants to stop the water of innocence from flowing downstream, first to Devon and then out to the shore via the salty, dirty Naguamsett.

Perhaps it's Leper's naivete that compels him to enlist before anyone else. When he sees the exciting film about the ski troopers, he decides this is a way he can join the war effort. The film offered a sanitized view of the war, so he grabbed the opportunity before he was drafted into a branch of the military where he would face the war head-on.

Chapter 10 begins with the narrator stepping outside of the story and offering perspective from an adult point of view: "That night I made for the first time the kind of journey which later became the monotonous routine of my life: traveling through an unknown countryside from one unknown settlement to another." He further explains that he went into uniform at the time when the USA's enemies were receding. He never fought. Instead, he trained and moved around the country to be ready for action, but his group was never needed. He also comments that the atomic bomb "seemed to have saved our lives."

We learn more about Gene's life after high school. This small glimpse informs readers that Gene does indeed join the military, but he never has to face battle. By letting the readers know about the future, the author creates dramatic irony. Gene, Brinker, Finny, and the other boys all feel apprehensive about the war. After the introduction to Chapter 10, however, the readers know that Gene never has to face fire from the enemy. In fact, his entire generation is a bit too young to face the worst of the war.

Gene travels to Vermont, and as soon as he hears Leper speak, he knows that something irreparable has happened. Leper tells Gene he sees a lot he never saw before. Some of those things are real, and some of them are hallucinations. The snow's crust represents Leper's mental state. It has the appearance of smoothness. It's bright and shiny. But under the weight of the boys' steps, it starts to crack. Gene says the cracking noises "sounded to my ears like rifles being fired in the distance." This simile compares the boys' serene surroundings to the war, and the comparison shows how much their worlds have merged. It seems that exposure to the war has caused Leper's mental breakdown. Gene can't handle the scene, and he flees back to Devon.

Lesson 10 Vocabulary

Look the following words up in a dictionary or online and learn their meanings and spellings:

monotonous

holocaust

draughty

aesthete

preliminary

querulous

modulate

plume

Lesson 10 Reading Quiz

1. How does Gene get to Vermont?

2. Who is standing in the window of the Lepellier home when Gene arrives?

3. With whom do Gene and Leper eat lunch?

4. What is a Section Eight discharge from the military?

5. Leper says the army turned everything "inside out." What is something he says is inside out?

Lesson 10 Short Essay Questions

1. In the telegram Leper sent, he tells Gene that he's at "Christmas location." Do you have a location you associate with a certain time of year? Write about that place and the associated time of year. How do you feel about that location when you're not there?

2. Compare Leper of the Beaver Dam to Leper of the Army. What has changed in him? Do you think he'll ever be the same again?

3. Leper tells Gene, "You always were a lord of the manor, weren't you? A swell guy, except when the chips were down. You always were a savage underneath. I always knew that only I never admitted it." Do you think Gene was always a savage underneath? Do you think this could be said of anyone? Why or why not?

LESSON 11

Reading Assignment

How has Gene's trip to Vermont changed him? Will everything be normal back at Devon?

Chapter 11 Summary

All Gene wants to do is see Phineas, and he finds him in the middle of a snowball fight at the Fields Beyond, close to the woods at the edge of the Devon School property. Finny gets Gene to join his team, but after some time, Finny starts throwing snowballs at everyone, regardless of their team. The fight ends with everyone ganging up on Finny, and he cheerfully surrenders.

Finny doesn't have to use a cane anymore. He has a walking cast. Still, Gene worries that he might be doing too much. After dinner, Phineas and Brinker want to hear about Leper. Gene tells them the truth about Leper, and then reality hits. "Now the facts were re-established, and gone were all the fantasies, such as the Olympic Games for A.D. 1944, closed before they had ever been opened."

The war completely takes over their lives. The boys start making preparations about which branch of the service to join. Gene, though, doesn't take action.

One day, Brinker confronts Gene about not enlisting. He accuses him of putting it off because he pities Finny. The way to get over it, Brinker says, is to clear everything up about the accident so they can all forget about it.

Gene has been helping Finny with his Latin so he can graduate. He explains a passage he's been translating for Finny. It's about a surprise attack on Caesar's army. Finny hates Latin and considers Caesar to be a tyrant over his life because he has to sit in classrooms and learn a dead language. Finny believes in things he learns firsthand,

and that's why he finally believes the war is real: he saw Leper with his own eyes and could tell he was crazy. "If a war can drive somebody crazy, then it's real, all right…" They laugh about their fantasies and hope that nobody else sees Leper while he's on campus.

At 10:05 that night, Brinker bursts into Gene and Finny's room and tells to get ready to go. They assume it's some kind of senior prank and go along with it. They're taken to the First Building where Brinker has arranged the Assembly Room to look like a court with ten members of the class in graduation robes as the jury.

Brinker uses a loud voice to introduce a trial to investigate Finny's accident. He says they need to put rumors and suspicions to rest. Brinker questions Finny, who says he simply fell out of the tree because he lost his balance. This is rejected because Finny never loses his balance. The boys go back and forth about the details of Finny's fall, and then someone remembers that Leper was there and always remembers details. Finny tells them that Leper is at Devon, and two boys leave to go find him.

Leper enjoys the attention he receives as Brinker questions him. He affirms that two boys were up in the tree, and he says they moved "like an engine," meaning one person moved first (like a piston) and then the other person fell down. Leper continues talking defiantly, not understanding the point of the conversation. He thinks they're talking about him, not about Finny and Gene.

Finny starts to leave, and Brinker asks him to wait until they have all the facts. Finny is crying now and yells at Brinker before leaving the room and going out to the corridor. That's when they hear him falling down the white marble stairs

Chapter 11 Analysis

The ugly, stark reality of Leper's mental illness sends Gene reeling, and all he wants is to retreat to Finny's fantasy world. He returns to Devon and finds Finny engaged in a snowball fight with the school's "best and brightest." They're at the far end of the school, up next to the woods: "I stood there wondering whether things weren't simpler and better at the northern terminus of these woods, a thousand miles due north into the wilderness, somewhere deep in the Arctic, where the peninsula of trees which began at Devon would end at last in an untouched grove of pine, austere and beautiful."

Gene continues: "There is no such grove, I know now, but the morning of my return to Devon I imagined that it might be just over the visible horizon, or the horizon after that." Gene still grasps at innocence, at childhood, at life before the war. But this chapter severs those illusions.

The next couple of scenes foreshadow what will happen later in the chapter. Finny has organized the snowball fight and carefully orchestrated the teams. But at the climax of the fight, he starts attacking everyone, friend and foe, and as a result, everyone turns on him. "Loyalties became hopelessly entangled. No one was going to win or lose after all... We ended the fight in the only way possible; all of us turned on Phineas. Slowly, with a steadily widening grin, he was driven down beneath a blizzard of snowballs."

Next, Gene translates a Latin text for Finny to help him pass a class, and they talk about an interesting passage regarding a surprise attack. The passage is confusing, but they summarize it by saying Caesar isn't doing well but ends up winning in the end. A surprise attack is about to happen to Finny, but does he end up winning in the end? Perhaps the *idea* of Finny ends up winning in the end.

The scene in the Assembly Hall is the climax of the story. The tone is dark and somber. No other scenes have been set in this location, so it's new and foreign to the reader. There's an odd mix of old and young, familiar and strange. Brinker uses the language of the very adult court system, but the students crack jokes about comic books. Just a few short months ago, Leper would have brought pure innocence with him upon entering the scene. But now, having been tainted by the war, he brings a surliness and self-interestedness that is new and dangerous. It's the same scene as the snowball fight, but this time it takes place in an adult setting, and Finny can't control the outcome.

Lesson 11 Vocabulary

Look the following words up in a dictionary or online and learn their meanings and spellings:

primeval

inveigle

vitality

plantation

resentment

infantile

fortitude

vestibule

grimace

Lesson 11 Reading Quiz

1. Who is the only person Gene wants to see after his visit to Leper?

2. What's going on in the Fields Beyond when Gene gets back to Devon?

3. Who are the two men in their class who are "sidelined for the Duration" that Brinker talks about?

4. What convinces Finny that a real war is on?

5. Who organizes the impromptu court hearing late at night in the Assembly Room?

Lesson 11 Short Essay Questions

1. Gene remarks, "Over my cot I had long ago taped pictures which together amounted to a barefaced lie about my background—weepingly romantic views of plantation mansions, moss-hung trees by moonlight, lazy roads winding dustily past the cabins of the Negroes. When asked about them I had acquired an accent appropriate to a town three states south of my own, and I had transmitted the impression, without actually stating it, that this was the old family place. But by now I no longer needed this vivid false identity; now I was acquiring, I felt, a sense of my own real authority and worth, I had had many new experiences and I was growing up." When you were younger did you have a "vivid false identity" that helped you until you had a sense of your own real authority and worth? Describe that identity and any experiences that allowed you to let it go.

2. "There was little left at Devon any more which had not been recruited for the war." What does this statement have to do with Brinker's impromptu court hearing? Is there any connection?

3. Leper compares Gene and Finny's movements on the tree branch to an engine with two pistons. Engine pistons can't move of their own accord. Do you think this is an accurate comparison?

LESSON 12

Reading Assignment

At this point in the novel, we're seeking resolution to the catastrophes that have come before. Will this chapter provide the denouement (the resolution to the climax)?

Chapter 12 Summary

Everyone springs into action, trying to make Finny comfortable and getting him the help he needs. Gene notes that each person, even Finny himself, remains calm and collected, keeping Finny still, finding adult help, and then transporting him to the Infirmary.

Through all of this action, Gene feels helpless. He hovers about the perimeter of the action but doesn't do anything truly helpful. He crouches outside the Infirmary window and listens to what's happening inside. He can't hear much, and he makes up conversations in his head, which cause him to laugh. He doesn't want to be heard, so he stifles his laughter and waits. When the adults have all gone away, Gene whispers into the room and Finny responds angrily, "You want to break something else in me! Is that why you're here!" Finny is so angry that he half falls off his bed and struggles to get back on. Gene says he's sorry and then walks away. He wanders aimlessly around the school and ends up sleeping under the stadium ramp.

In the morning, he returns to his room to get his notebook and finds a note from Dr. Stanpole: "Please bring some of Finny's clothes and his toilet things to the Infirmary." Gene packs some of Finny's things into his suitcase and takes them to the Infirmary.

Finny seems unfriendly when he arrives. He then tells Gene that he spent all winter writing letters to all the branches of the military to find a way he could serve in the war. As soon as he got a positive response, he planned on admitting the war was real.

Gene tells Finny that he wouldn't have been any good in the war, even if nothing had happened to his leg. They would have put him in the front somewhere, and soon he would be making friends with the Germans or the Japanese, and the war would be a terrible mess.

Finny begins to cry and asks if it was just some blind impulse that caused him to shake the tree branch. He forgives Gene.

The rest of the day passes quickly. Dr. Stanpole tells Gene to return to the Infirmary at 5 o'clock when Finny will be coming out of anesthesia after having his bone set. Gene has a productive, successful day and arrives at the Infirmary at 4:45. Dr. Stanpole seems distraught. He sits down next to Gene and says, "This is something I think boys of your generation are going to see a lot of." He tells him Finny died during the surgery. His heart stopped without warning. The only explanation, Dr. Stanpole says, is that a piece of bone marrow "must have escaped into his blood stream and gone directly to his heart and stopped it."

Chapter 12 Analysis

Up until Chapter 12, Gene and Finny have never directly discussed the incident in the tree. Brinker tries to force them to face the issue, but his efforts lead to a new crisis. When Finny is finally alone in the Infirmary after falling down the marble stairs, he feels very angry with Gene. But the next day, the two friends reconcile. After their talk, they both seem content.

All along, Finny has denied the reality of the war because it couldn't be real for him. As soon as he could make it real (by finding a way to serve) he planned on admitting it was real. He never could find a way, however; it's as if he couldn't exist in a warring world. It was incompatible with his nature.

Gene explains this to Finny by saying it wouldn't have worked even if his leg had been fine. Instead of fighting, Finny would have turned the enemies into friends.

In the end, Finny forgives Gene by saying, "I believe you. It's okay because I understand and I believe you. You've already shown me and I believe you."

Finny's death is caused by a piece of his bone marrow travelling from his leg to his heart. Marrow often symbolizes vibrant, healthful living. Bone marrow is the life-giving substance that nourishes our bones. Finny himself is a life force, always bringing joy and energy to any situation. If we think back to the beginning of the book when Finny organized the Super Suicide Squad, we could almost say that Finny's body committed suicide when he realized he was incompatible with a world of war.

Lesson 12 Vocabulary

Look the following words up in a dictionary or online and learn their meanings and spellings:

repressed

pontiff

irreconcilable

maladjustment

decrepit

animosity

parody

languid

Lesson 12 Reading Quiz

1. What is Finny's new injury from falling down the stairs?

2. Who keeps talking about "the old college try"?

3. Where does Gene sleep the night Finny falls down the stairs?

4. Why has Phineas been writing letters to various branches of the military?

5. What happens when Dr. Stanpole sets Finny's bone?

Lesson 12 Short Essay Questions

1. Phil Latham wraps a blanket around Finny after he falls down the stairs. Gene says, "I would have liked very much to have done that myself; it would have meant a lot to me. But Phineas might begin to curse me with every word he knew, he might lose his head completely, he would certainly be worse off for it. So I kept out of the way." Do you think Gene is right that Phineas wouldn't want his help? Why or why not?

2. Write a farewell letter from Gene to Finny. Write all the things you think Gene would have wanted to say to Finny if he had the chance.

3. Dr. Stanpole says to Gene, "This is something I think boys of your generation are going to see a lot of, and I will have to tell you about it now." Write about the boys of Gene and Finny's generation and what the next few years will be like for them. How would your generation be changed if you had to go through the same experiences as the 1943 class of Devon School?

LESSON 13

Reading Assignment

We readers have been left with a shock. We need some closure to help us tie up the mental and emotional loose ends. Finish reading the novel.

Chapter 13 Summary

The boys have graduated, and they're packing up their belongings. At the same time, Jeeps, troops, and sewing machines flood the Far Quadrangle. Devon will become the Army Air Force's Parachute Riggers' school for the duration.

Brinker's father visits with Brinker and Gene in the Butt Room. A veteran of World War I, Brinker's father wishes he were young enough to be a part of the current war. He reproves the boys for trying to stay out of harm's way, reminding them that they'll be asked about their war experiences for the rest of their lives.

Gene goes to the gym to clean out his locker. A platoon undresses in the locker room as he gathers his belongings. In just a few weeks, Gene will enter the military himself, and his life will be as regimented as the lives of the parachute riggers who are moving into Devon School.

Gene reflects that only Phineas was never afraid and never hated anyone. Quackenbush struck out at the menace; Brinker developed a general resentment. Leper gave up the struggle absolutely. The novel ends with Gene's reflections on whether the enemy is even an enemy at all.

Chapter 13 Analysis

The transformation from innocence to experience is now complete. Phineas is gone, and the troops have moved in to Devon School. Gene's generation is now transitioning to the war.

In literature, a microcosm is a representation of something on a much smaller scale. It means "small world." In *A Separate Peace*, Devon is a microcosm for the world at large (the macrocosm). During the summer term, the boys of Devon existed in a peaceful, idyllic setting, even though the world was at war. In many ways, America spent the early years of World War II much like the boys at Devon. While the rest of the world was at war, America continued its existence, seemingly unaware of the chaos in other parts of the world. In both cases, a violent act awakened the naïve parties. In the microcosm, a friend's careless impulse resulted in the shattering of Finny's leg. In the macrocosm, the bombing of Pearl Harbor woke a "sleeping giant."

In the last three paragraphs of Chapter 13, Gene remarks on the war's effects on several of the characters. Mr. Ludsbury reacted to the war with belligerence. Quackenbush struck out at it randomly. Brinker developed a careless general resentment against the war. And Leper faces it directly and then gives up the struggle absolutely. Only Phineas remained strong, carefully allowing himself to face the war only as he knew he could handle it.

Gene, being an extension of his friend, absorbed Finny's strength. He never had to kills anyone in the war, and he never developed an intense hatred for the enemy. In the end he wonders if the enemy is an enemy at all.

He seems to have accepted his role in Finny's death: "He possessed an extra vigor, a heightened confidence in himself, a serene capacity for affection which saved him. Nothing as he was growing up at home, nothing at Devon, nothing even about the war had broken his harmonious and natural unity. So at last I had."

At the end of *A Separate Peace*, the tone is serious and philosophical. The author leaves his readers with heavy questions to ponder. What is peace? Who is an enemy? What does it mean to forgive? What is the value of a life?

Lesson 13 Vocabulary

Look the following words up in a dictionary or online and learn their meanings and spellings:

quadrangle

gyration

cogitation

cordiality

vitality

erratic

assimilate

rigger

calisthenics

Lesson 13 Reading Quiz

1. What does Gene see out on the Far Common from the window in his room?

2. Why are the troops unloading sewing machines?

3. Whose father wants to meet Gene?

4. Why does Gene go to the gym?

5. Which character, according to Gene, was never afraid?

Lesson 13 Short Essay Questions

1. Gene watches the troops move into Devon as the students move out. They appear busy and regimented. Gene says, "Around them spread a beautiful New England day. Peace lay on Devon like a blessing, the summer's peace, the reprieve, New Hampshire's response to all the cogitation and deadness of winter. There could be no urgency in work during such summers; any parachutes rigged would be no more effective than napkins." Can you think of a place in your life that seems so peaceful that no emergency or commotion could ever unsettle it? What makes it so peaceful?

2. Brinker often blames his parents' generation for the war. From the conversation in the Butt Room, can you identify two differences between Brinker's father's generation and the boys' generation? Write about the differences, and then write about three similarities between the generations.

3. A Maginot Line is an elaborate, permanent defensive barrier (it was invented by André Maginot, a French war minister from the early 20th century). Gene says, "All of them, all except Phineas, constructed at infinite cost to themselves these Maginot Lines against this enemy they thought they saw across the frontier, this enemy who never attacked that way—if he ever attacked at all; if he was indeed the enemy." What has Gene learned about reacting to outside forces? How did Phineas avoid building Maginot Lines at infinite cost to himself?

LITERARY DEVICES AND TERMS

Identifying the use of common literary devices helps the reader to understand the story on a deeper level. It's helpful to talk about just a few literary devices at a time. For instance, on any given reading assignment, maybe just talk about point of view, figurative language, and theme. Unless your students are well-acquainted with literary devices, they might feel overwhelmed by the task of "analyzing" so much. To really learn about literary devices, talk about the same devices for several units in a row. You could spend a whole semester focusing on symbolism and allusion by studying specific instances of these literary devices in several different texts. Definitions for the literary devices below are written in italics, and the specific examples from this text are explained afterward.

Point of View

Point of view depicts the manner in which a story is narrated by who it is that tells the story. In first-person narrative, the story is told by a narrator who is also a character within the story. You can recognize first-person point of view by the words "I" or "we." First-person point of view gives the author a chance to convey the narrator's thoughts and feelings in an intimate way. Second-person point of view is rarely used in fiction because the narrator refers to the reader as "you." It's a very direct manner of writing, and it's more frequently employed in self-help non-fiction. Third-person point of view offers the author the greatest flexibility, so it's the most commonly used narrative mode in literature. In the third-person point of view, each character is referred to as "he," "she," "they," or "it," but never as "I" or "we," except in dialogue. Authors have two options when using the third-person point of view. They can allow the narrator to be "omniscient," meaning that the narrator knows everything that's going on in the story, or the narrator can be "limited," knowing only what's going on from a single character's perspective.

The author of *A Separate Peace* uses the first person point of view, and Gene Forrester is the narrator. At several points throughout the novel, Gene speaks to us from an adult perspective, as a man returning to the school he attended fifteen years earlier. At these points, the tone is reflective, and Gene gives us additional information that we haven't yet received from the narrative. For instance, when Gene travels to Leper's home in Vermont, he tells us that he would soon take many late-night train rides like this while serving in the military.

Through most of the story, however, Gene tells the story from a teenager's perspective. When speaking from his younger perspective, Gene is a somewhat unreliable narrator. Because of his youth and his emotional attachment to Phineas, his perceptions can't be completely trusted. Unreliable narrators keep readers highly engaged because they have to act like detectives to figure out what is really going on.

Tone

A literary work's tone is the attitude the author adopts toward a specific character, place, development, or idea. Tone can render a variety of emotions ranging from frightening, serious, and critical to witty, light-hearted, and humorous. Readers can usually ascertain the author's feelings towards a topic by the tone, and this understanding influences the meaning of the story.

The tone of *A Separate Peace* is mostly dark. Right from the start, when Gene walks around the Devon School after having been away for fifteen years, he mentions "fear's echo." It's foggy outside, threatening to rain, and the old tree seems "weary from age, enfeebled, dry."

At times, the tone changes to nostalgic, especially when the narrator recalls happy times. Descriptions of Phineas carry the warm feeling of nostalgia: "Under the influence not I know of the hardest cider but of his own inner joy at life for a moment as it recaptured that magic gift for existing primarily in space, one foot conceding briefly to gravity its rights before spinning him off again into the air. It was his wildest demonstration of himself, or himself in the kind of world he loved; it was his choreography of peace." The shifts in tone illustrate Gene's feelings about his friend. The world is sunny when Finny is in his element; darkness comes when Finny is hurt or gone.

Imagery

Imagery is a literary device authors employ to create mental images for the reader. In fiction, imagery is one of the most powerful tools at a writer's disposal because it elicits sensory perceptions in the reader. Common forms of imagery include metaphors, allusions, descriptive words, and similes.

John Knowles uses rich imagery to help us visualize the setting, the characters, and the actions in A *Separate Peace*. Let's take the following passage as an example:

As I had to do whenever I glimpsed this river, I thought of Phineas. Not of the tree and pain, but of one of his favorite tricks, Phineas in exaltation, balancing on one foot on the prow of a canoe like a river god, his raised arms invoking the air to support him, face transfigured, body a complex set of balances and compensations, each muscle aligned in perfection with all the others to maintain this supreme fantasy of achievement, his skin glowing from immersions, his whole body hanging between river and sky as though he had transcended gravity and might by gently pushing upward with his foot glide a little way higher and remain suspended in space, encompassing all the glory of the summer and offering it to the sky."

In this long, long sentence, the author compares Phineas to a god. He compares his body to a complex set of balances. He describes the way his skin glows and how Phineas concentrates on his feat with intensity.

Foreshadowing

The literary device foreshadowing refers to the use of words, phrases, or images that hint at what will later unfold in the story. Foreshadowing gives the reader hints without revealing the story or spoiling the suspense. Wise use of foreshadowing suggests an outcome to the story without making the reader feel that the hinted outcome is inevitable.

At the beginning of the novel, Gene explains that he went back to the Devon School and walked around the buildings and grounds. He recounts his visit much as a tour guide would expound a place's history to visitors, but certain details foreshadow events we'll read about later in the story.

For instance, Gene talks about "a long white marble flight of stairs." It seems strange that he would talk about the "exceptional hardness" of the marble. He also talks about the tree next to the Devon River. He describes the tree as a giant from his childhood. To him, the tree appears "weary from age, enfeebled, dry." All of his initial observations foreshadow events to come, and we expect these events to be ominous from the tone of his hints.

Protagonist

In literature, the protagonist is the main character of a story who ends up in conflict because of the antagonist. The protagonist is also the character that the readers are most likely to identify with.

Gene Forrester is the protagonist of *A Separate Peace*, and it's easy for readers to relate to him. We all feel jealous of others at times, and we long to fit in with our peers. Gene is also the narrator, but he's not a terribly reliable narrator. He tells the story from fifteen years in the future. Much has happened since the events of 1942-1943, and his memory is clouded by nostalgia, regret, and time.

Antagonist

The antagonist in a literary work represents the opposition against the protagonist. The antagonist may be another character in the story, but sometimes the antagonist is a group of characters, an institution, or even nature itself. In classic stories, the antagonist was the villain who tormented the hero (the protagonist). The antagonist is often used to create the conflict within the story.

A *Separate Peace* is a coming-of-age story, and the main antagonist is the war. While the boys sometimes see each other as enemies, their biggest enemy is the wider world and the war that will soon recruit them for service.

At the end of the novel, Gene talks about some of characters' enemies (or antagonists). Mr. Ludsbury hated anything that threatened him. Quackenbush hated anyone who appeared to be a rival. Brinker resented the war and its demands on his life. Leper feared the unknown and the outside world. Gene reflects: "All of them, all except Phineas, constructed at infinite cost to themselves these Maginot Lines against this enemy they thought they saw across the frontier, this enemy who never attacked that way—if he ever attacked at all; if he was indeed the enemy" (see page 87 for more on the Maginot Lines).

Gene must learn to overcome his own insecurities and guilt. When Finny forgives him in the infirmary, Gene gains the equilibrium to move forward and face the future.

Irony

Irony is a difference or contrast between appearance and reality. In other words, it's a discrepancy between what appears to be true and what is really true. In literature, there are three common types of irony: verbal irony, situational irony, and dramatic irony. In verbal irony, characters say the opposite of what they mean (for example, a character may be condemned by a speaker pretending to praise him). In situational irony, a situation is different from what common sense indicates it currently is, what it will be, or what it ought to be. Situational irony is often used to expose injustice. Dramatic irony occurs when a character states something she believes to be true, but the reader knows it is not true. Dramatic irony is often used in mysteries to increase dramatic tension.

By letting the readers know about the future, the author creates dramatic irony in *A Separate Peace*. Gene, Brinker, Finny, and the other boys all feel apprehensive about the war. After the introduction to Chapter 10, however, the readers know that Gene never has to face fire from the enemy. In fact, his entire generation is a bit too young to face the worst of the war.

The name of the "Super Suicide Society of the Summer Session" is ironic as well. The name, conceived in humor and good fun, ends up describing the result of the summer session: the death of Finny. In fact, Finny's own bone marrow is what kills him in the end.

Narrator Gene remarks on the situational irony observed in the scene after Finny's second injury. The boys and men carry Finny on a chair: "People aren't ordinarily carried in chairs in New Hampshire, and as they raised him up he looked very strange to me, like some tragic and exalted personage, a stricken pontiff." By nature, Finny is someone who carries others. He brought everyone together during the summer session. He organized the winter carnival. He got everyone to turn on him during the snowball fight so they could be united. It's ironic to see him being carried by others.

Metaphors

The purpose of a metaphor is to take a concept the reader understands clearly and use it to better understand a lesser known element. In fiction, authors employ metaphors to describe scenes, characters, and actions in such a way that the reader can see, feel, and understand the story. The most common method of using metaphors is to say that one thing is another thing: "He was eager to help but his legs were rubber." In this metaphor, the author, Raymond Chandler, gives the reader a thorough description in just a few words by telling us the character's legs "were rubber."

John Knowles uses an extended metaphor to help readers understand the impact of the war: "So the war swept over like a wave at the seashore, gathering power and size as it bore on us, overwhelming in its rush, seemingly inescapable, and then at the last moment eluded by a word from Phineas; I had simply ducked, that was all, and the wave's concentrated power had hurtled harmlessly overhead, no doubt throwing others roughly up on the beach, but leaving me peaceably treading water as before. I did not stop to think that one wave is inevitably followed by another even larger and more powerful, when the tide is coming in."

Similes

Like metaphors, similes also make comparisons between two unrelated or dissimilar things for the sake of creating a deeper understanding. The difference between similes and metaphors is that similes use the words "as," "such as," or "like" in drawing the connection. In Les Miserables, *Victor Hugo wrote, "There was a quivering in the grass which seemed like the departure of souls." This simile not only gives the reader a stunning mental image, but it also helps to set the tone for the scene.*

The author uses a simile in his vivid description of the film that convinces Leper to enlist: "Skiers in white shrouds winged down virgin slopes, **silent as angels,** and then, realistically, herringboned up again, but herringboned in cheerful, sunburned bands, with clear eyes and white teeth and chests full of vigor-laden mountain air."

Later, after Gene has witnessed Leper's post-military mental state, he describes the sound of the ice and trees cracking: "The two sharp groups of noises sounded to my ears like rifles being fired in the distance." By comparing the sounds to rifles being fired, Gene connects Leper's breakdown with his time in the military.

Personification

Personification is a figure of speech in which animals or objects are given human characteristics. This literary device is extremely common in children's literature where animals talk and houses look out at all the people. Personification is often used to describe something vividly or to emphasize a point. The following sentences use personification to describe a scene: "The ocean danced in the moonlight." "The avalanche devoured everything in its path."

In Chapter 10, Gene sees "the sun rejoicing on the snow." His own feelings about springtime affect the way he describes the scene.

Back at the beginning of the novel, it's interesting to see the way the author describes the tree. Fifteen-years-older Gene sees it as "weary from age, enfeebled, dry." These are all words we might use to describe a very old person. Just a couple of paragraphs later, however, we encounter a flashback. Sixteen-year-old Gene describes the very same tree quite differently: "The tree was tremendous, an irate, steely black steeple beside the river." Although this second reference isn't an example of personification, it's interesting to see the contrast between the two descriptions of the same subject.

Allusion

In literature, an allusion is a figure of speech that makes reference to people, places, events, literary works, myths, or works of art. Generally, it's left to the reader to make the connection, thus providing a deeper level of meaning to the literary work. The following sentence is an example of allusion: "Sally had a smile that rivaled that of the Mona Lisa." Everyone knows what the Mona Lisa's smile looks like, so the author employs that common knowledge in describing his own character. The most common allusions stem from the Bible, Shakespeare, and Greek and Roman mythology.

Most of the allusions in *A Separate Peace* stem from classical education, which matches the environment of the Devon School. The author also mentions songs that were popular in the 1940s such as "Don't Sit Under the Apple Tree" and "They're Either Too Young or Too Old."

The boys are familiar with Thomas Hardy's novels, Virgil, Moliere, and Voltaire. When describing the campus, Gene says, "The school had been largely rebuilt with a massive bequest from an oil family some years before in a peculiar style of Puritan grandeur, as though Versailles had been modified from the needs of a Sunday school." Versaille is the opulent palace of King Louis the IV of France.

Symbolism

Symbolism may take several different forms in literature. It gives a literary work more richness and color, and it can be used to represent more abstract ideas. In addition, authors often use symbolism to suggest a mood or emotion; through symbolism, the mood or emotion can be suggested instead of blatantly revealed. Symbolism can be found in colors (white for life and purity), objects (chain links for unity), flowers (violets for shyness), and many other objects or attributes.

The two rivers that straddle the Devon school are symbols. By learning about these symbols early in the story, the entire plot makes more sense and takes on more meaning.

The Devon is a narrow little river with a "thick fringe of pine and birch." It's a freshwater river, and its source lies just up the hill. When Gene sees the Devon, he thinks of "Phineas in exaltation, balancing on one foot on the prow of a canoe like a river god, his raised arms invoking the air to support him, face transfigured, body a complex set of balances and compensation…" The Devon is small, clean, and completely understood. It's predictable and safe. It's a symbol of youth and safety.

The Naguamsett, on the other hand, is "ugly, saline, fringed with marsh, mud and seaweed." It joins with the ocean, "so that its movements [are] governed by unimaginable factors like the Gulf Stream, the Polar Ice Cap, and the moon." It symbolizes adulthood and the unknown.

Youth is inevitably followed by adulthood, as the rivers suggest: "The Devon's course was determined by some familiar hills a little inland; it rose among highland farms and forests which we knew, passed at the end of its course through the school grounds, and then threw itself with little spectacle over a small waterfall beside the diving dam, and into the turbid Naguamsett."

Finny's cast serves as a symbol of reality. "Then my eyes fell on the bound and cast white mass pointing at me, and as it was always to do, it brought me down out of Finny's world of invention, down again as I had fallen after awakening that morning, down to reality, to the facts." Phineas has a knack for making people forget about harsh realities, but that doesn't mean they're gone.

Theme

A theme is a central dominating idea that acts as a foundation for an entire literary piece. The theme is not the same as the "moral of the story"; rather, it is the meaning released by the work when we take all aspects of the work in its entirety into account. There may be more than one theme to a literary work; in fact, this is often the case. To discover a work's theme, ask yourself the following questions: What kind of people does the story deal with? Are the characters in control of their lives, or are they controlled by fate? Why do the characters behave as they do? How does the author perceive reality? What is the author's attitude toward the subject? What are the values of the characters in the story? What values does the author seem to promote?

There are at least three potential themes in *A Separate Peace*: Growing Up, Identity, and Enmity.

Growing Up: When the novel begins, Gene, Finny, Leper, and the other summer session attendees balance their time between school and playing, but they definitely tip the scales toward play. Finny cajoles Gene out of studying to jump in the river or play Blitzkrieg. They spend their sparkling summer days in or near the Devon River, which symbolizes childhood and innocence. After Finny's accident, the fall session begins, and Gene finds himself in a different world. He's thrown into the Naguamsett during his fight with Quackenbush, and the war seems to encroach from every angle. Leper, who exemplified innocence and naivete during the summer session, enlists and suffers a mental breakdown. The boys try to hang on to childhood and innocence with Finny's help (as seen during their winter carnival and subsequent snowball fight), but when Finny dies, childhood and innocence are irrevocably lost.

Identity: Gene struggle with his own identity through much of *A Separate Peace*. During the summer session, he feels jealous of Finny's easy-going confidence and wants to be like him. He knows he can't match Finny's physical prowess, so he works on emphasizing his own academic prowess. In the scene after Finny's fall, Gene dresses in Finny's clothes and marvels at how much he looks like his friend. From this point on, Gene and Finny depend on one another psychologically; it's as if their identities begin to be blurred. Finny even starts to live vicariously through Gene, training him for the 1944 Olympics as he would have done himself. At the end, Gene feels as though he's attended his own funeral. As an adult, he reestablishes his own identity, recognizing Finny's unique and exemplary traits and feeling grateful for the way Finny helped him through the journey to adulthood.

Enmity: "Enmity" isn't a word we use often, but it perfectly describes one of the themes in *A Separate Peace.* Enmity is "the state or feeling of being actively opposed or hostile to someone or something." At the end of the novel, adult Gene points out that every character has "constructed at infinite cost to themselves" defenses against the enemy. But these enemies never attacked, and in the end, one has to wonder if the enemy ever existed at all. Phineas is the one character who never seems to experience jealousy, resentment, anger, or fear. Ultimately, he helps Gene to see that it's possible to live without the negativity that results from distancing yourself from your fellow humans.

END-OF-UNIT PROJECT OPTIONS

Essay

Write a five-paragraph essay about the symbolism of the two rivers in *A Separate Peace*. Explain what each of the rivers represents, and use concrete details from the novel to back up your assertions.

Ecology Project

Leper Lepellier collected snails and tracked the habits of local beavers. Choose an animal that lives in your area, and learn everything you can about it. What kinds of tracks does it leave? How long does it live? How does it care for its young? When are the times of day you're most likely to see one? Feel free to use the Internet, books, and YouTube for background information, but spend most of your time doing firsthand research. How much can you learn from simple observation? Keep a notebook for recording what you learn and share it with your teacher or a parent.

Athletic Brochure

You're trying to get blitzball recognized as an official Olympic sport. Create a trifold brochure that explains the sport. List all of the rules. It's true that the rules have been in dispute. You'll have to make some judgment calls when laying them out in black and white.

Include a diagram of a blitzball field so the Olympic officials know what kind of stadium to construct. Propose a design for blitzball uniforms so that country delegations can prepare their athletes. You may also want to include a proposed training schedule for blitzball athletes.

Mapmaking

Create a 3D map of the Devon School using any materials you wish. For ideas, you might look at the website for Phillips Exeter Academy, which is the boarding school attended by author John Knowles in the 1940s. Include a guide showing where various events took place (the Winter Carnival, Gene's early-morning Olympic training, the fight with Cliff Quackenbush, meetings of the Super Suicide Society of the Summer Session, etc.).

History Project

The students at Devon had to learn to make their own beds when maid service disappeared "for the duration." In the rest of the USA, families had to learn how to deal with rationing.

Research the twenty items rationed during the war. Find out why each one was rationed and what innovative substitutes were developed to fill their places. You might even find recipes developed during the war with substitutes for rationed ingredients.

Share your findings by creating a poster, brochure, blog post, Power Point presentation, or other display of your choice.

Art Project

When Gene and Finny ride bicycles to the ocean, Gene sees dawn for the first time. Here's how he describes it: "Very gradually, like one instrument after another being tentatively rehearsed, beacons of color began to pierce the sky. The ocean perked up a little from the reflection of these colored slivers in the sky. Bright high lights shone on the tips of waves, and beneath its gray surface I could see lurking a deep midnight green. The beach shed its deadness and became a spectral gray-white, then more white than gray, and finally it was totally white and stainless, as pure as the shores of Eden." Use your favorite art medium to turn Gene's description into a visual piece of art.

ANSWER KEY FOR READING QUIZZES

Lesson 1

1. It's been 15 years since the narrator has been to the Devon School.
2. Devon is located in New Hampshire/New England.
3. The narrator is looking for a particular tree.
4. It's Finny's idea to jump from the tree into the river.
5. They miss dinner.

Lesson 2

1. Mr. Prud'Homme is dressed in a gray business suit. Most of the other Devon Masters dress more "British" and careless.
2. The shirt Phineas receives from his mother is pink.
3. Phineas is excited that America has bombed Central Europe.
4. The story takes place in 1942.
5. Phineas and the narrator cement their partnership by jumping together into the river from the tree.

Lesson 3

1. The Super Suicide Society of the Summer Session meets every night.

2. Gene never misses club meetings.
3. There are no teams in blitzball.
4. A. Hopkins Parker is the holder of the 100-meter freestyle swim record at Devon School.
5. Gene has a big test in the morning, he hates long bicycle rides, and he knows they risk expulsion.

Lesson 4

1. They don't eat breakfast because Phineas lost their seventy-five cents.
2. Gene flunks his test.
3. Mr. Prud'Homme is interested in hearing about their trip to the beach, and he doesn't punish them.
4. Gene gets angry because he's trying to study for his French exam.
5. He jumps into the river.

Lesson 5

1. Gene wears Finny's pink shirt.
2. Dr. Stanpole advises Gene to be cheerful and hopeful but to help Phineas accept that sports are over for him.
3. Gene tells Finny the story about a grass fire behind their house that they try to put out with flaming brooms.
4. Gene tells Finny that he jounced the branch on purpose.
5. No, Gene is already a day late getting back to Devon.

Lesson 6

1. Leper lived across the hall from Finny and Gene during the summer session.
2. The Devon is a small, fresh-water river, and the Naguamsett is a dirty, saline river affected by the tides.
3. Gene's last name is Forrester.
4. Cliff Quackenbush is the manager of the crew team.
5. Finny calls to make sure Gene saves his place for him in his room.

STUDY GUIDE: A SEPARATE PEACE

Lesson 7

1. Brinker Hadley is tall and straight and he has substantial buttocks. He's outgoing and confident.
2. The Butt Room is a room in the basement where the boys like to smoke.
3. The Devon students pick local apples because of the worker shortage.
4. Leper is looking for a beaver dam.
5. They go to the train station to help shovel out a train that is stuck in the snow.

Lesson 8

1. Phineas gives Brinker Hadley his new nickname.
2. Devon is dangerous for Finny because the walkways are icy and slippery.
3. Finny thinks the war isn't real.
4. Phineas wants Gene to compete in the 1944 Olympic Games.
5. Mr. Ludsbury is thin.

Lesson 9

1. Leper is the first member of the class to enlist.
2. Saturday afternoons are terrible.
3. Phineas creates the Winter Carnival.
4. Phineas sacrifices a copy of the *Iliad* in order to have a fire.
5. The telegram is from Leper.

Lesson 10

1. Gene takes a train to Vermont.
2. Leper is standing in the window when Gene arrives.
3. Gene and Leper eat lunch with Leper's mother.
4. A Section Eight discharge means you're not mentally fit for the armed forces.
5. Answers could include any of the following: the man coughing next to him, not being able to sleep at night but sleeping everywhere during the day, being hungry everywhere except the Mess Hall.

Lesson 11

1. Gene only wants to see Phineas.
2. There is a snowball fight in the Fields Beyond when Gene returns from Vermont.
3. The two sidelined men are Leper and Phineas.
4. Seeing Leper back at Devon convinces Finny that a real war is on.
5. Brinker organizes the impromptu court hearing.

Lesson 12

1. Finny rebreaks his leg when he falls down the stairs.
2. Phil Latham talks about "the old college try."
3. Gene sleeps under the stadium.
4. Phineas has been trying to find a military branch that will let him serve in the war.
5. A piece of bone marrow travels to Finny's heart and kills him.

Lesson 13

1. Gene sees Jeeps and troops assembling on the quadrangle.
2. The troops will be making parachutes.
3. Brinker's father wants to meet Gene.
4. Gene goes to the gym to clean out his locker.
5. Phineas was never afraid.

WHICH TOLMAN HALL LITERATURE UNIT STUDY WILL YOU USE NEXT?

Onion John by Joseph Krumgold

Number the Stars by Lois Lowry

Princess Academy by Shannon Hale

Two Old Women by Velma Wallace

The Creature Department by Robert Paul Weston

Moon Over Manifest by Clare Vanderpool

Crispin by Avi

Roll of Thunder, Hear My Cry by Mildred D. Taylor

PUT THE JOY BACK IN WRITING WITH TOLMAN HALL'S JUST WRITE! MIDDLE SCHOOL WRITING PROMPTS

How will your students improve their writing? By writing, of course! This workbook makes writing comfortable and fun by providing 150 interesting writing prompts, which are accompanied by 150 intriguing photographs. With the visual help and a written headstart, your students won't have to stare off into space before connecting their pens with the paper. Give your students an opportunity to write a little each day in a no-stress situation, and soon they'll see writing as a valuable tool instead of an intimidating demand.

WELCOME TO THE FAMILY!

Keep up with the latest news, book lists, author interviews, book reviews, and new study guide releases by signing up for our email newsletter at
www.tolmanhall.com

Please leave a review for this Tolman Hall Literature Unit Study at Amazon, Barnes & Noble, Smashwords, Goodreads, or Kobo. Thanks for your support!

ABOUT THE AUTHOR

Rachel Tolman Terry holds a B.A. in English from Brigham Young University and has been a professional writer and author since 1998. Her work has appeared in numerous magazines including *The Old Schoolhouse* and *Practical Homeschooling*. She has homeschooled her three children and tutored other children in their literature studies. To schedule speaking engagements, ask questions, or give suggestions for books for future *Tolman Hall Homeschool Literature Unit Studies*, contact Rachel at tolmanterry@gmail.com or visit www.racheltolmanterry.com.
Follow Rachel on Twitter @_rachelterry_

Made in the USA
Las Vegas, NV
24 August 2021